Quack!

Written by Matthew Benjamin
Illustrated by Kristen Goeters

Three little ducks,
one, two, three.

Quick, little ducks,
swim here to me.

3

Three little ducks
as quiet as can be.

Quick, little ducks,
swim here to me.

6

Three quick ducks
all swimming back.

Quack, quack, quack, quack,
quack, quack, quack!

Three little ducks, one, two, three.

8   Quick, little ducks, swim here to me.